CHRISTMAS

ADULT COLORING BOOK

Asshole

Vol.1

SWEAR WORD AND MANDALAS

COLOR TEST PAGE

COLOR TEST PAGE

fucktard

FANNY

Fuck Off

Bitch

Slag

Lameass

Bollocks

Assface

Pussy

Fuck

Fucking!

Bitch

Douche

Piss Flaps

Cunt

Dickhead

arsehole

Shitballs

Bellend

Holy Shit

Tosser

Bastard

FUCK THAT SHIT

MERRY CHRISTMAS
DIPSHIT

Holy
Shit

Damn

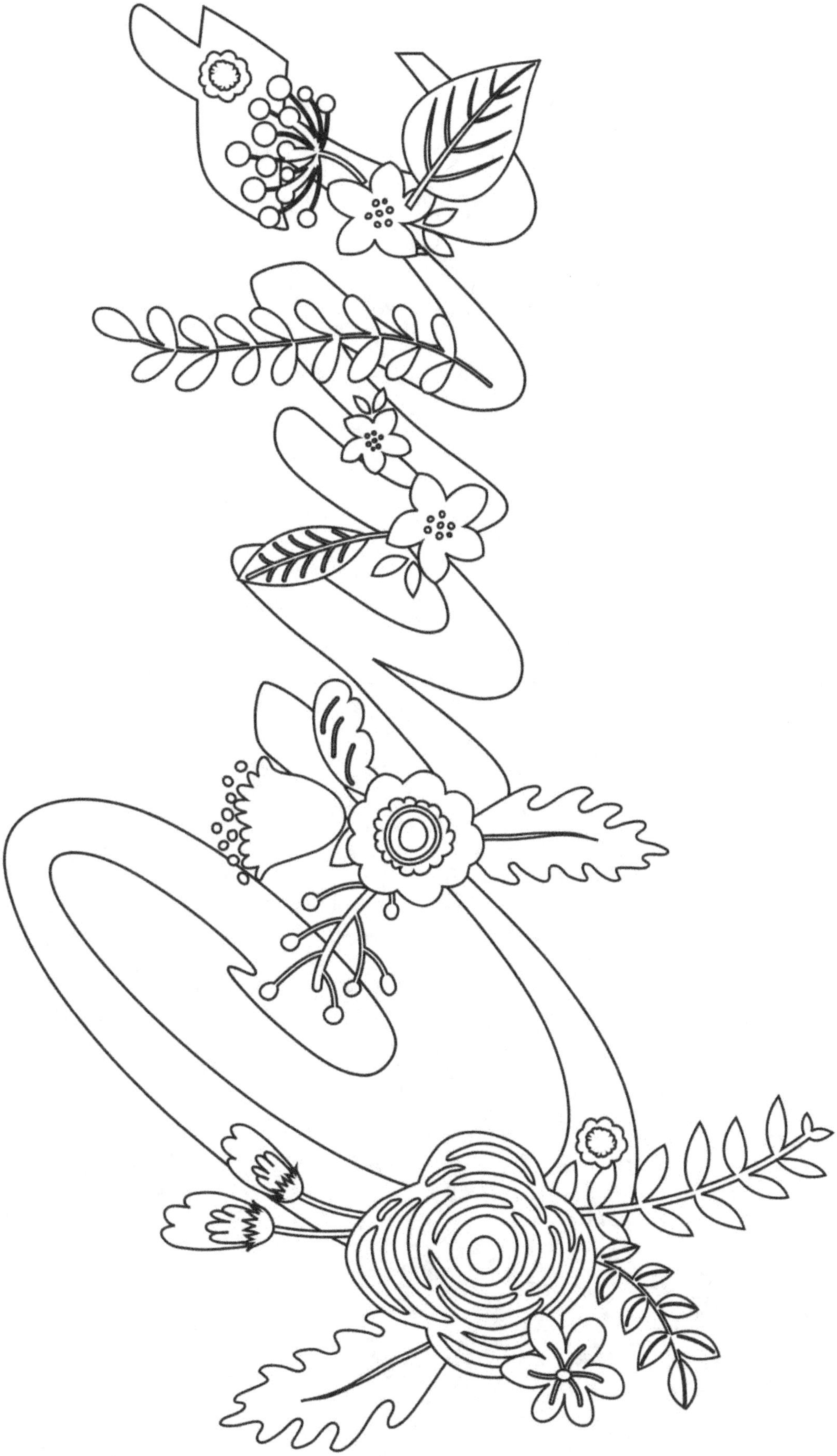

Idiot

www.ingramcontent.com/pod-product-compliance
Lightning Source LLC
Chambersburg PA
CBHW081747280526
45789CB00008B/2770
* 9 7 8 1 5 3 9 9 4 4 1 1 9 *